SNAKES

Anacondas

by Linda George

Consultants:
The staff of Black Hills Reptile Gardens
Rapid City, South Dakota

COPY 2
**CAPSTONE
HIGH-INTEREST
BOOKS**

an imprint of Capstone Press
Mankato, Minnesota

Capstone High-Interest Books are published by Capstone Press
151 Good Counsel Drive, P.O. Box 669, Mankato, Minnesota 56002
http://www.capstone-press.com

Library of Congress Cataloging-in-Publication Data
George, Linda.
    Anacondas/by Linda George.
    p.cm.—(Snakes)
    Includes bibliographical references and index (p.48).
    ISBN 0-7368-0907-4
    1. Anaconda—Juvenile literature. [1. Anaconda. 2. Snakes.] I. Title.
II. Animals and the environment. Snakes.
QL666.O63 G46   2002
597.96'7—dc21   2001000045

Summary: Describes the physical attributes, habitat, and hunting and mating methods
of anacondas.

Editorial Credits
Blake Hoena, editor; Lois Wallentine, product planning editor; Timothy Halldin, cover
    designer and illustrator; Katy Kudela, photo researcher

Photo Credits
Cheryl A. Ertelt, cover, 16–17, 34, 44
Francois Gohier, 12, 26, 29, 37, 41
Joe McDonald, 15, 18
Joe McDonald/Visuals Unlimited, 6, 22
Laurie Grassel, 10
Mark Newman/Visuals Unlimited, 25
William Holmstrom, 9, 21, 30, 33
W. Perry Conway/TOM STACK & ASSOCIATES, 38

Table of Contents

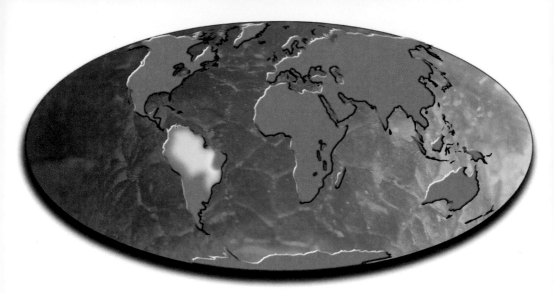

Yellow represents the anaconda's range.

Fast Facts about Anacondas

Scientific Names: There are three species of Anacondas. These species are *Eunectes murinus, Eunectes notaeus,* and *Eunectes deschauenseei.*

Size: Anacondas are the heaviest snakes in the world. They may weigh more than 200 pounds (90 kilograms) in the wild. Anacondas also are one of the longest snakes. They can grow to be more than 20 feet (6 meters) long.

Range:	Anacondas live in northern and central South America. They most often are found near the Amazon and Orinoco Rivers. These areas include the countries of Brazil, Columbia, and Venezuela.
Food:	Anacondas eat fish, birds, small mammals, and reptiles.
Habitat:	People sometimes call anacondas "water boas." Anacondas spend much of their time in the water. Anacondas live in marshes and swamps. They also live near rivers and streams.
Habits:	Anacondas are constrictors. They kill prey by squeezing it. Snake experts believe that anacondas are ill-tempered. Anacondas often bite handlers.
Reproduction:	Anacondas are ovoviviparous. Their eggs develop and hatch inside the female's body. The female then gives live birth to her young. A female anaconda will give birth to a clutch of 20 to 40 young.

CHAPTER 1

Anacondas

Anacondas are the heaviest snakes in the world. They may weigh more than 200 pounds (90 kilograms) in the wild. In captivity, they may grow to weigh more than 300 pounds (140 kilograms).

Anacondas also arc one of the longest snakes. Only reticulated pythons grow longer. Anacondas can grow to be more than 20 feet (6 meters) long.

Herpetologist William Lamar recorded finding one of the longest anacondas in the wild. Herpetologists are scientists who study reptiles and amphibians. In 1978, Lamar

Anacondas are one of the largest snakes in the world.

found an anaconda that was 24 feet, 7 inches (7.5 meters) long. He found this snake in Columbia, South America.

Snake Families

Snakes are reptiles. Alligators, crocodiles, lizards, and turtles also are reptiles.

More than 2,300 snake species exist in the world. A species is a specific type of animal or plant. Scientists divide snake species with similar features into families. Anacondas are members of the Boidae family. Snakes in this scientific group are constrictors. They squeeze their prey to death. The Boidae family also includes boas and pythons.

Scientists divide the Boidae family into two subfamilies. These groups include the Pythoninae and the Boidnae subfamilies.

Snakes in these subfamilies are closely related. But they have one main difference. Pythons are oviparous. Female pythons lay eggs that develop and hatch outside their body. Boas and anacondas are ovoviviparous. Their

Anacondas are constrictors.

eggs develop and hatch inside the female's body. Female boas and anacondas then give live birth to their young.

Scientists further divide snake families into genera. Anacondas are members of the *Eunectes* genus. This genus includes three species of anacondas.

Anacondas, boas, and pythons have spurs.

Primitive Snakes
Scientists consider anacondas, boas, and pythons to be primitive snakes. Scientists believe that these snakes are not as developed as other snake species. They still possess traits similar to their lizard ancestors.

Anacondas, boas, and pythons have two developed lungs. They use both of their lungs to breathe. Most other snake species have a small left lung and a developed right lung. These snakes use their right lung to breathe. This lung also is elongated. It may be as long as half of a snake's body. A single, elongated lung better fits in a snake's long, narrow body than two developed lungs do.

Anacondas, boas, and pythons also have traces of hind limbs and a pelvis. This hip bone is attached to two femurs. On anacondas, boas, and pythons, these leg bones appear as small claws called "spurs." The spurs are most visible on male snakes. More developed snakes do not have these traces of hind legs.

CHAPTER 2

Anaconda Species

Three species of anacondas exist. These species are *Eunectes murinus*, *Eunectes notaeus*, and *Eunectes deschauenseei*.

Green Anacondas

Eunectes murinus is the scientific name for green anacondas. Green anacondas are the largest anaconda species. Their average length is between 10 and 20 feet (3 and 6 meters). They may grow to weigh more than 200 pounds (90 kilograms).

Green anacondas are brown-green, olive, or gray-green in color. Dark brown or black, oval spots cover their body. The spots on their

Green anacondas are the largest anaconda species.

sides are yellow in the middle. Green anacondas have a yellow or cream colored underbelly. They have dark stripes running from their eyes to their upper jaw.

Yellow Anacondas

Eunectes notaeus is the scientific name for yellow anacondas. They are smaller than green anacondas. Yellow anacondas usually do not grow to be longer than 10 to 12 feet (3 to 3.7 meters). They usually weigh less than 100 pounds (45 kilograms).

Yellow anacondas look similar to green anacondas. They also have spots similar to green anacondas. But yellow anacondas' skin is a shade of yellow, gold, or yellow-green.

Marajo Island Anacondas

Eunectes deschauenseei is the scientific name for dark-spotted or Marajo Island anacondas. This species of anaconda is similar in size and appearance to yellow anacondas.

A yellow anaconda's skin is a shade of yellow.

Marajo Island anacondas are very rare. Little is known about them. Few scientists have studied this anaconda species.

Head

Side Spots

Green Anaconda

Oval Spots

CHAPTER 3

Habitat

People sometimes call anacondas "water boas." Anacondas spend a great deal of time in the water. Anacondas often are found near the Amazon and Orinoco Rivers in South America. These areas include the countries of Brazil, Columbia, and Venezuela.

Living in Water

Anacondas move slowly on land because of their large size. They seem to prefer being in the water. Anacondas' bodies are buoyant in water. Water supports their heavy weight.

Anacondas sometimes are called water boas because they spend a great deal of time in the water.

Anacondas' bodies are well suited for swimming. Their eyes and nostrils are on top of their head. This positioning helps anacondas see and breathe while they swim. Anacondas swim with their body almost completely underwater. Anacondas also can hold their breath for long periods of time while swimming underwater.

Habitats

Green anacondas live in tropical South America. They live east of the Andes Mountains and as far south as Bolivia. They also live in northern Paraguay. Green anacondas live in swamps and marshes. They also live in and around the Amazon River.

Yellow anacondas can be found in northern Argentina, Paraguay, southeastern Bolivia, and Brazil. They live in swamps, marshes, and slow-moving rivers and streams.

Anacondas swim with most of their body underwater.

Marajo Island anacondas live in the Marajo Island region of Brazil. This island is located in northeastern Brazil. It is between the Amazon and Para Rivers.

CHAPTER 4

Hunting

Anacondas are carnivores. They eat other animals. Anacondas eat birds and small mammals. They also eat fish and reptiles such as turtles and lizards. They even eat small alligators called caimans. Some large anacondas can eat pigs and deer.

Hunting

Anacondas are nocturnal. They are most active at night. They often rest along river banks or in swamps and marshes during the day.

Anacondas ambush their prey. They hide near the edge of rivers and streams. They then wait for prey to come to the water and drink.

Anacondas hide and ambush their prey.

Anacondas also hide in the weeds of swamps and marshes. Anacondas' coloring helps to camouflage them. This coloring blends with their natural surroundings. Animals often do not see anacondas until they strike.

Senses for Hunting

Anacondas cannot see well. But they are able to detect shapes and movement. This ability helps them find prey.

Anacondas cannot hear sounds as people do. Instead, they feel vibrations in the ground, air, or water. These sensations help anacondas know when prey is near.

The Jacobson's organ is located on the roof of an anaconda's mouth. Snakes use this organ to smell. An anaconda flicks out its tongue to collect scent particles in the air and on the ground. The tongue carries the scents to the Jacobson's organ. An anaconda can smell prey with its Jacobson's organ.

Anacondas use their tongue to help them smell.

Anacondas constrict their prey.

A male anaconda can smell females that are
ready to mate.

Constriction
An anaconda strikes when prey is near. Its
teeth curve toward the back of its mouth. This
shape helps an anaconda hold onto prey as it
struggles to escape.

After catching an animal, an anaconda kills its prey through constriction. The anaconda wraps its muscular body around its prey. But an anaconda does not crush the prey and break its bones. Instead, an anaconda squeezes each time its prey breathes out. This prevents the animal from taking another breath. It may take an anaconda only minutes to suffocate small prey such as rodents and birds. But an anaconda may struggle with larger prey such as caimans for more than an hour.

Many scientists believe constriction affects the circulatory system. Constriction prevents the heart from pumping blood to the body. Heart failure also may cause an anaconda's prey to die.

An anaconda sometimes drowns its prey The snake grabs its prey and pulls it underwater.

Eating

An anaconda swallows its prey whole. It may take an anaconda several hours to swallow large prey.

An anaconda most often swallows prey head first. This positioning makes it easier for an anaconda to swallow its prey. The prey's limbs then fold neatly against the body.

An anaconda can swallow prey that is much larger than its mouth. Ligaments connect its upper and lower jaws. These stretchy bands of tissue allow an anaconda's jaws to separate as it swallows prey.

An anaconda moves its head back and forth to move the prey into its mouth. This action also separates its jaws. An anaconda's strong throat muscles then pull the prey into its stomach.

Digesting Food

Strong acids within an anaconda's stomach digest prey. These chemicals break down food to be used by the body. An anaconda can digest almost every part of their prey except for its hair and teeth. It even can digest bones.

Anacondas rest while their food digests. The weight of prey in their stomach makes it

Anacondas often rest after eating.

difficult for them to move. After eating, anacondas also need to use their energy to digest their food. It may take anacondas several days or weeks to digest large prey.

Anacondas do not need to eat often. After a large meal, they may go several months to a year without eating.

CHAPTER 5

Mating

Anacondas give off a strong-smelling secretion. Some scientists believe that this substance's scent may help anacondas find each other during the mating season.

Breeding Balls

Anacondas form a breeding ball during mating. Two to 12 males coil themselves around a female. The males may stay wrapped around the female for two to four weeks.

Scientists are not exactly sure how this type of mating works. They are not sure if one or more of the males in the breeding ball actually mates with the female. Some scientists plan

Anacondas form a breeding ball when they mate.

to study a group of newborn anacondas. They want to find out if all young anacondas in a clutch have the same father or if they have different fathers.

Birth

Female anacondas often are inactive while pregnant. They do not move around much. They may not eat while pregnant. They often lie in the sun to warm their body. The warmth helps keep their eggs warm. Eggs need warmth to develop and survive.

Anacondas are ovoviviparous. Their eggs develop and hatch inside the female's body. Female anacondas then give live birth to their young.

Female anacondas give birth six to eight months after mating. A clutch of anacondas may include 20 to 40 young snakes. Young anacondas may be 2 feet (.6 meter) long or longer at birth. Their length depends on the size of their mother. Larger females give birth to larger young.

The size of young anacondas at birth depends on the size of their mother.

Female anacondas do not take care of their young. Young anacondas crawl or swim away on their own after birth. They are able to find prey on their own.

CHAPTER 6

Anacondas and People

A common myth exists about a group of explorers traveling through the jungles of South America. The explorers came to a green wall that was too high to climb. It seemed to go on forever in both directions. They walked down the wall for days. They hoped to find a gate through the wall. Instead, they found the head of a giant anaconda. The wall really was a giant snake.

Many myths are told about anacondas. These false stories often tell of extremely large snakes. In the early 1900s, British army officer

Many myths are told about anacondas.

Lieutenant Colonel Percy Fawcett reported finding a 62-foot (19-meter) anaconda in southern Brazil. In 1948, a newspaper in Rio de Janeiro, Brazil, told of an anaconda that knocked over buildings. People said the snake was more than 150 feet (46 meters) long. But there are no photographs or scientific proof to support these claims. In truth, anacondas rarely grow to be more than 20 feet (6 meters) long.

In 1910, U.S. President Theodore Roosevelt offered a reward of $1,000. He offered this reward to anyone who captured a live snake that measured more than 30 feet (9 meters). Over the years, the reward has increased to $50,000. It is now offered by the Wildlife Conservation Society. The reward remains uncollected to this day.

Anaconda Legends

A snake believed to be an anaconda is in a 2,000-year-old Arawak Indian painting. These native people lived in South America. They believed snakes were powerful beings.

The Carib Indians of South America tell several stories about how their people were

Anacondas do not hunt and kill animals that they cannot swallow.

created. In one story, an anaconda was chopped into thousands of pieces. Each piece of this snake then became a Carib Indian.

Early Spanish settlers in South America referred to anacondas as "Matatoro." This word means "bull killer." The settlers believed anacondas killed full-grown cattle.

Some people believe that anacondas may attack and eat people. But most people are too

Anacondas often try to swim away from danger.

large for anacondas to eat. Anacondas do not hunt animals that they cannot eat.

Defenses

Anacondas have few natural predators. Their size and strength prevents other animals from hunting them as food. Large predatory birds may eat young anacondas. Caimans also may eat young anacondas.

Anacondas move slowly on land. They are not able to flee quickly when they feel threatened. An engorged anaconda sometimes will regurgitate partially digested food. After vomiting its food, the anaconda can move more easily to try and escape. Anacondas also can swim away from danger when in the water.

Snake experts believe that anacondas are ill-tempered. These snakes often bite when handled. Anacondas also bite to defend themselves. Their bites do not kill. But they can seriously injure a person.

Dangers to Anacondas

Some people hunt anacondas. Anaconda skins can be used to make shoes, purses, and belts. Thousands of anacondas are killed each year for their skins.

Ranchers are afraid that anacondas may kill their farm animals. These people shoot anacondas that they see on their land.

Anacondas also are sold as pets. Most South American countries do not allow anacondas to be captured and sold as pets. But people smuggle anacondas out of these countries and sell them illegally. Most snake experts believe that anacondas do not make good pets. Anacondas often bite their handlers.

Scientists currently do not know a great deal about anacondas. They hope to study how anacondas mate. Scientists also want to know how many anacondas live in the wild. They want to learn if anacondas are in danger of extinction.

Most scientists believe that anacondas are not in danger of dying out. Anacondas are good at hiding and sometimes are difficult to find. Their strength and hunting abilities also help them survive.

Scientists are trying to learn more about anacondas.

Words to Know

acids (ASS-ids)—substances in an animal's stomach that help it break down food

camouflage (KAM-uh-flahzh)—coloring or covering that makes animals, people, and objects look like their surroundings

carnivore (KAR-nuh-vor)—an animal that eats meat

clutch (KLUHCH)—a group of newly born snakes

digest (dye-JEST)—to break down food so that it can be used by the body

family (FAM-uh-lee)—a group of animals with similar features

femur (FEE-mur)—the large upper leg bone

habitat (HAB-uh-tat)—the place and natural conditions in which plants and animals live

herpetologist (hur-puh-TAH-luh-gist)—a scientist who studies reptiles and amphibians

nocturnal (nok-TUR-nuhl)—active at night

ovoviviparous (oh-voh-vye-VIP-ah-rus)—having eggs that develop and hatch inside the female's body; ovoviviparous animals give live birth to their young.

pelvis (PEL-viss)—the area of an animal that includes the hip bones

predator (PRED-uh-tur)—an animal that hunts other animals for food

prey (PRAY)—an animal hunted by another animal for food

primitive (PRI-muh-tiv)—relating to an early stage of development; scientists believe anacondas are a primitive species of snake.

regurgitate (ree-GUR-juh-tate)—to vomit food

species (SPEE-sheez)—a specific type of animal or plant

To Learn More

Mattison, Christopher. *Snake*. New York:
DK Publishing, 1999.

McDonald, Mary Ann. *Anacondas*.
Chanhassen, Minn.: Child's World, 1999.

Murphy, John C., and Robert W. Henderson.
*Tales of Giant Snakes: A Historical Natural
History of Anacondas and Pythons.*
Malabar, Fla.: Krieger Publishing, 1997.

Steele, Christy. *Anacondas*. Animals of the
Rain Forest. Austin, Texas: Steadwell
Books, 2000.

Welsbacher, Anne. *Anaconda*. Predators
in the Wild. Mankato, Minn: Capstone
High-Interest Books, 2001.

Useful Addresses

Black Hills Reptile Gardens
P.O. Box 620
Rapid City, SD 57709

Milwaukee Public Museum
Herpetology Department
800 West Wells Street
Milwaukee, WI 53233-1478

National Zoological Park
3001 Connecticut Avenue NW
Washington, DC 20008

Toronto Zoo
361A Old Firch Avenue
Scarborough, ON M1B 5K7
Canada

Internet Sites

Black Hills Reptile Gardens
http://www.reptile-gardens.com

Enchanted Learning.com-Anacondas
http://www.EnchantedLearning.com/subjects/
reptiles/snakes/Anacondacoloring.shtml

Nashville Zoo-Anaconda
http://www.nashvillezoo.org/anaconda.htm

Toronto Zoo
http://www.torontozoo.com

Index